I0048629

What's My Potential Exposure to Estate Taxes?

Summarizing Data Your Accountant Needs to Estimate Your Estate Taxes

Teresa M. O'Brien

Disclaimer

This book is not meant to replace IRS Form 706, which is a very in-depth form, but is to help guide my readers into how to summarize the information for calculating the Estate Taxes they may owe. Like most government forms, Form 706 is in the Public Domain, and I have utilized some of their descriptive text.

Copyright © November, 2021 Teresa M. O'Brien

All rights reserved. This book or any portion thereof may not be reproduced or used in any manner whatsoever without the express written permission of the publisher except for the use of brief quotations in a book review.

ISBN: 978-1-7379432-1-1

First printing, 2021.

O'Brien Consulting Group, LLC
Midland, MI 48640

TABLE OF CONTENTS

INTRODUCTION

When a person dies, all assets titled in his/her name, become part of his/her estate. The federal government and some state governments impose taxes on estates valued at higher than an established minimum.

The threshold for having to pay federal Estate Taxes in calendar year 2021 is $11.7 million per individual with a top estate tax rate of 40%. The $11.7 million per individual is the highest threshold in the last 25 years (except for 2010 when there was none that year.)

There are currently discussions to lower the federal exemption threshold, although the exact amount is not yet known. What is known is that if no legislative action is taken between now and January 1, 2026, the federal estate tax exemption will revert to what it was in 2017, plus an adjustment for inflation. In 2017 the threshold was approximately $5.5 million – less than half of what it is today. An adjustment for inflation might bring that number to around $6 million. While that is still a fairly large number, if you start adding in death benefits of annuities and insurance, estate values can grow quite quickly.

If no legislative intervention happens before January 1, 2026, the top estate tax rate will go from 40% currently to 45%. Your tax advisors will be able to tell you your relevant state government estate tax thresholds and tax rates.

Estate taxes and income taxes are not the same. Income taxes are paid on your net *income,* while estate taxes are generated based on the value of the *net assets* in your estate. The value of your assets for estate tax is calculated differently than how you calculate your net worth. For example, estate taxes use the *death* benefit value of insurance and annuities, not the *surrender* value which would be used in calculating net worth.

A beneficiary is generally not taxed on the life insurance funds received. Instead, the value of the death benefit of a life insurance policy is considered an *asset* in the decedent's estate when completing IRS Form 706 for Estate and Generation Skipping Taxes. Assets that are transferred to a spouse are handled differently (marital deduction) than those that are transferred to a non-spouse.

So, it pays to have your accountant or tax advisors figure out periodically what your estate tax exposure might be in various state and federal tax scenarios using the information you provide in this book. The answer may be that you need to do nothing (yeah!) but it is worth having the discussion with your key tax advisors periodically so they can better support you. This can also be an opportunity to have a broad, strategic discussion with your accountant and tax advisors.

Your tax advisors can provide you only an e*stimate* of your estate tax position. An actual estate tax is calculated based on a decedent's date of death. Since you are still living, no one can give you an *exact* value for your estate taxes. At the time of death, your accountant will need further precision, details, and supporting documentation to complete an actual IRS Form 706 and accurately calculate your actual taxes.

The purpose of this book is NOT to give you tax advice. That's the responsibility of your tax advisors. This book is about getting your information organized so you can have a knowledgeable discussion with your accountant and tax advisors. It's really about bringing an overview of your total asset picture for your advisors to review. Form 706 is quite cumbersome to wade through so I have created the tables in this book to help organize your information in a more accessible format.

How to use this book:

I have organized this book in the order of what is required in IRS Form 706 for reporting Estate and Generation Skipping Taxes. Submitting your asset information in this order will make it easier for your accountant to enter your information into IRS Form 706 to give you an estimate of your federal estate tax exposure and – if applicable - your state estate tax exposure.

Fill in the information on the attached pages as best you can. Be particularly careful with insurance and annuity items because the *death* benefit that is required on Form 706 may be significantly higher than the *surrender* value that you use in figuring your net worth.

Your accountant will want to discuss your listed assets with you to determine which ones might have special allowances, which could reduce your exposure to estate taxes. To expedite those discussions, be as specific as possible when describing your assets, ownership, value, and beneficiaries.

Because you are using this information only to *estimate* your estate's exposure to taxes at some future date, there is no need to add small amounts of money individually to these tables. For example, a checking account with a $200 balance and a CD of $1000 will not impact the analysis of your potential estate taxes when the threshold is greater than $5.5 million. So, lump all those small valued accounts together and enter just one combined value.

Since estate taxes are calculated for an individual, each spouse should complete a separate set of worksheets.

DATA FOR ESTIMATING
TOTAL GROSS ESTATE

Real Estate Information

There are 3 ways each of us can own assets: (1) individually, (2) jointly with only our spouse, and (3) jointly with any others (including companies). **Include in this table only real estate that is owned SOLELY by you**. Certain farm and closely held business property can be valued at its special-use value.

Description (address, property type – i.e. house, land, etc.)	Current Value

Stocks and Bonds Information

In this table list only stock and bonds that are SOLELY OWNED by you. Include both retirement plans accounts and non-retirement accounts.

Description (Institution, account type, content (e.g. stock)	Total Current Account Value

Mortgages, Promissory Notes Payable TO You, and Cash Information

This table is for debt that others owe to only you. This includes mortgages, promissory notes, and contracts to sell land.

Mortgage and Notes Payable TO You

Description (Property and type of debt)	Sale Price	Purchaser's Name	Payoff Date	Unpaid Balance

Cash

This table is only for cash that you alone own. For institutions where you have relatively <u>small</u> amounts of cash, you can just sum up the total amount of cash that you hold at each institution, rather than listing all the sub-accounts.

Financial Institution	Account Number	Type of Account*	Total Value

*Types of accounts can include checking, savings, CD, etc.

Life Insurance

This can be for insurance on your life, for the benefit of your estate, or if you have the power to change the beneficiary, surrender or cancel the policy, assign or revoke the assignment of the policy, pledge the policy for a loan, can get a loan from the insurer for the surrender value of the policy, or if there is a reversion of interest.

Make sure to include any key person insurance, if the beneficiary is your spouse or a company that you own in whole or in part. In valuing your estate, the ***death benefit*** number is the one that is used.

Description – include name of institution and policy number	Owned By	Beneficiary	Death Benefit

Jointly-Owned Property and Interests

This is for property that only you and your spouse own jointly. This includes those assets held in joint tenancy and those held in tenants by the entirety.

List all property, of whatever kind, whether real estate, personal property or bank accounts – if you have joint tenancy with right of survivorship or as a by the entirety.

Description	How Held	Property Total Value

All Other Jointly Owned Interests

List any property and assets you own with others, beyond just your spouse.

Property Description	Co-Owners	YOUR % Ownership	Property TOTAL Value

Other Miscellaneous Property Not Reported Elsewhere

This is only for assets solely owned by you. Jointly owned assets should be listed on pages 9 and 10. In this section include any debts due you that weren't previously listed, such as any interest in a business, Archer Medical Savings Accounts (MSA), health savings accounts (HSA), rights, royalties, leaseholds, judgments, household goods and personal effects estimates, shares in trust funds, farm products and crops, livestock, farm machinery, automobiles, interest in a partnership, or an unincorporated business.

Description	Current Value

Any Transfers of Estate Already Made by You During Your Lifetime (beyond the annual per person exclusion amount)

Also include here any transfers with a retained life estate, transfers taking effect at death, and any revocable trust transfers. Note the amount of gift tax that is still payable on gifts that you have already made $_____.

Transfers Already Made	When Transferred	Value at Transfer

Power of Appointment Property

This table is for property that a deceased person, in their will, has designated you as the owner, to distribute as outlined via their will, which you have not yet distributed. An example might be "I give to Mary all my vinyl records to be divided equally among her and her siblings". If you, Mary, have possession of the records but haven't yet distributed them, then the value of the records would be listed here.

Property Description	Current Value

Annuities

In general, you must include in the gross estate all or part of the value of any annuity if (1) the contract/agreement was entered into after March 3, 1931, (2) it is receivable by a beneficiary after your death because they are your survivor, and (3) the annuity is payable to you (or you have the right to receive the annuity) either alone or in conjunction with another for your life or for a period that doesn't end before your life, or for any period that doesn't reference your death.

Make sure to use the *death benefit* value, not the surrender value. For purposes of calculating your ownership percentage, any part of the premium initially paid by your employer is calculated as though paid by you. Do NOT include Social Security benefits.

Description (Note if the annuity is inside an IRA)	Initial Purchase Percent Paid by You*	Owned By	Beneficiary	Death Benefit Value

*You and/or your employer

DATA FOR ESTIMATING
ALLOWABLE DEDUCTIONS

Debts, Mortgages, and Liens Payable BY You

List here any debts secured by a mortgage or a lien on the property of your gross estate. Property taxes accrued, income taxes accrued, and accrued business expenses are deductible, as are debts. If these accruals are small relative to the rest of your debts, these accruals can be lumped together for purposes of *estimating* your potential exposure to estate taxes.

Description Name of institution being paid, terms of debt	For which property	Initial Loan Value	Unpaid Balance	Payoff Date

Bequests to Surviving Spouse
(Marital Deduction)

List those bequests that *only your surviving spouse will get* as an heir, legatee, devisee, donee, surviving tenant by the entirety, joint tenant, as an appointee under decedent's exercise of power, beneficiary of decedents insurance of life, takes under dower or curtesy interest, or transferee of transfer made in decedent's lifetime.

Do not include (1) any property that isn't passing from you to your surviving spouse, (2) any property you haven't claimed as part of your gross estate, and (3) any property interest disclaimed by your spouse. If a deduction on a property has already been claimed in the table on page 16, then enter only the net value of property here (gross value – previous deduction). Because the marital deduction that is allowed varies whether your spouse is a US citizen or not, please indicate here the citizenship of your spouse _____.

Description of Property	Current Value

Charitable and other Gifts and Bequests as Part of Will

List here any gifts and bequests you intend to make to various organizations. Your accountant can then discuss with you which are allowable deductions for estimating your estate taxes.

Potential charitable deduction items include funds to corporations or associations organized and operated exclusively for religious, charitable, scientific, literary, or educational purposes (such as the arts or amateur competitive sports), the prevention of cruelty to animals or children, veteran organizations, and Indian tribal governments.

It can also be claimed if the recipient is the US, a state, a political subdivision of a state, or the District of Columbia, for exclusively public use. Donations to fraternal associations operating under the lodge system are also allowed if the funds are to be used exclusively for the previously listed purposes in the paragraph above. Also included are gifts and bequests to veterans organizations incorporated by Act of Congress, employee stock option transfers, transfers to Indian tribal governments.

Charity (Name and Description)	Description of What is Being Gifted	Current Value of Gift

Qualified Conservation Easement

Land qualifies if (1) it has been owned for at least 3 years, (2) the land is located in the US or its possessions, and (3) a qualified conservation easement on the land has been made.

Description of Land	Consideration Received for Easement	Charitable Deduction Already Made on This Land	Value of Any Developmental Rights Retained by You	Your Percent Ownership	Gross Value of Land

Deceased Spousal Unused Exclusion (DSUE) Amount From Pre-Deceased Spouse

If you are a surviving spouse, your accountant will want to discuss this further with you, including the Deceased Spouse Unused Exclusion (DSUE) –– the amount of unused exclusion transferred to you as a surviving spouse (if your spouse died after December 3, 2010).

Deceased's Name	Date of Death	DSUE Amount Received	DSUE Amount Applied to Lifetime Gifts	Remaining DSUE Amount

DATA FOR ESTIMATING OTHER TAXES

Generation Skipping Transfer Tax Payable by the Estate

IRS Form 706 is also used to calculate any generation skipping tax. This is an additional tax that would need to be paid only on items that are subject to estate tax and are to be transferred to a skip person. A skip person is 2 or more generations below you (e.g., your grandchild).

Description of Property or Items to be Transferred	Beneficiary & Relationship to You	Ownership % of Transfer Asset	Current Value Total Asset

Other Financial Workbooks by Teresa

Situation	Solution	QR Code and URL to Amazon Book Page
Widow or widower settling their deceased spouse's estate	*Now What Do I Do? Settling Your Spouse's Estate – Organizing and Simplifying the Process*	https://qrs.ly/mxe03gh
Friend or loved one settling estate of a person who was single at time of death	*The Estate Settler's Organizer – For Settling an Unmarried Friend or Family Member's Estate*	https://qrs.ly/2ge03hu
Summary of financial and other key information of a married couple (with or without dependent children)	*Our Money Summary – Summary of Family's Finances*	https://qrs.ly/7de03h8
Summary of financial and other key information for an unmarried adult (including recent graduate, widow, divorced, and with or without children)	*My Money Summary – Summary of My Personal Finances*	https://qrs.ly/o6e03ic
Outlining your income, expenses, and savings now & in future, so your financial planner can estimate if you will have enough money for your retirement	*Estimating Your Money Gap – Providing for Retirement*	https://qrs.ly/mbe03gu
Summarizing key personal and business information for a single, solo business owner, in case of emergency	*Business and Personal Information Summary - for the Single Small Business Owner*	https://qrs.ly/bge03i7

Your Opinion Is Important

It will help me improve this book and help other readers know what to expect.

If you have an Amazon account, you can scan the QR code below or use the URL to leave a review. *You may be requested to log in to your Amazon account to complete the review form.*

Let me know what you liked best, what was missing, if there was anything you would leave out, or anything else that's on your mind about the book.

Thanks!

https://qrs.ly/6oe1bk9

www.ingramcontent.com/pod-product-compliance
Lightning Source LLC
Chambersburg PA
CBHW051802200326
41597CB00025B/4657